MAR 2009

WITHDRAWN

DATE DUE			

MAJESTIC HORSES

APPALOOSAS

by Pamela Dell

Published in the United States of America by The Child's World®
PO Box 326 • Chanhassen, MN 55317-0326
800-599-READ • www.childsworld.com

PHOTO CREDITS
© blickwinkel/Alamy: 2
© Corbis: 16
© The Granger Collection, New York: 15
© Greg Philpott/Alamy: 12, 21
© Jonathan Blair/Corbis: 23
© Juniors Bildarchiv/Alamy: cover, 1, 4, 7
© Mark J. Barrett/Alamy: 11, 19, 25, 26

ACKNOWLEDGMENTS
The Child's World®: Mary Berendes, Publishing Director;
Katherine Stevenson, Editor

Content Adviser: Weezee

The Design Lab: Kathleen Petelinsek, Design and Page Production

LIBRARY OF CONGRESS CATALOGING-IN-PUBLICATION DATA
Dell, Pamela.
  Appaloosas / by Pamela Dell.
    p. cm. — (Majestic horses)
  Includes bibliographical references and index.
  ISBN 1-59296-780-9 (library bound : alk. paper)
  1. Appaloosa horse—Juvenile literature. I. Title. II. Series.
  SF293.A7D45 2007
  636.1'3—dc22   2006022643

TABLE OF CONTENTS

★ ★ ★ HORSES OF THE WEST

Sometimes you can feel an Appaloosa's spots! In winter, the spots sometimes have longer hair.

A horse comes racing across the Idaho plain. It is quick, strong, and sure-footed. It can climb rocky hillsides easily. Its coat has bright, bold spots. What is this powerful spotted horse? It is an Appaloosa.

This **breed** once carried Native Americans on buffalo hunts. But by the late 1800s, America's Appaloosas were almost all gone. Luckily, some lived on. Today, Appaloosas live in many parts of the world. Their special look makes them one of America's best-known breeds.

◀ This Appaloosa is carrying its rider through the desert sand.

★ ★ ★ WHAT DO APPALOOSAS LOOK LIKE?

Appaloosas come in many colors. Some are white, cream, or gray. Others are brown, **bay**, black, or **roan**. But Appaloosas are best known for their spots. The spots are different sizes and shapes. They show up in different places, too. Some Appaloosas have spots all over. Others have them only in certain places. Some Appaloosas have lots and lots of spots! Others have only a few spots—or none at all.

People have given names to the patterns of spots. A big patch of white over the back and hips is a *blanket*. It looks like a blanket thrown over the horse.

Some Appaloosas have plain white blankets. Others have blankets with spots.

This Appaloosa has spots all over! This type of coloring is called a leopard pattern. ▶

Many Appaloosas have dark and light stripes on their hooves.

Some Appaloosas have a *leopard* pattern. They are white, with dark spots. *Snowflake* Appaloosas are just the opposite. They are dark, with light spots. *Marble* Appaloosas are light colored, with really tiny dark spots. *Frost* Appaloosas are dark, with tiny light spots.

Appaloosas have spots on their skin, too! In fact, they are known for their **mottled** skin. The skin is pink with dark dots. You can see it around their noses and mouths.

◀ This is Appaloosa has a marble pattern. You can see the mottled skin on his nose.

Appaloosas' eyes are different, too. Most horses have eyes that look all dark. On people's eyes, you can see white around the outside. You can see the white on an Appaloosa's eyes, too.

A horse's height is measured from its **withers** to the ground. Appaloosas measure about 57 to 61 inches (145 to 155 centimeters). They are not very heavy horses. Most of them weigh 950 to 1,175 pounds (430 to 530 kilograms).

People often use the word *hands* to say how tall a horse is. A hand is 4 inches (10 centimeters). Appaloosas are about 14 or 15 hands high.

This Appaloosa lives on a horse farm. He has a blanket pattern. ▶

★ ★ ★ NEWBORN APPALOOSAS

Appaloosa foals can look very different from their parents. And spots and colors sometimes change as the horses age.

Newborn Appaloosa **foals** have long, skinny legs. But they can stand up soon after they are born. The mother keeps a close watch on her foal. The foal drinks its mother's milk to grow strong. After a while, it starts eating other foods.

Appaloosa foals sometimes change color as they grow up. Lighter-colored foals often get darker when they lose their baby hair. Gray foals get lighter as they grow.

◄ This Appaloosa mother is getting to know her new foal.

Appaloosas became a breed in America. But spotted horses lived in other lands much earlier. People have drawn pictures of spotted horses for thousands of years. These **ancient** spotted horses were not Appaloosas. Europe and Asia had many types of horses. Some of them happened to have spots.

North and South America had no horses when Europeans arrived. Some of the Europeans' horses got loose. Native Americans quickly put them to use. They traded them from one group to another. Some Native groups made horses a big part of their lives.

In ancient China, spotted horses were valued. An important book talked about "heavenly horses." People thought these might be spotted horses.

This drawing of a horse is from a cave in France. It is about 30,000 years old! Some early drawings show spotted horses. ▶

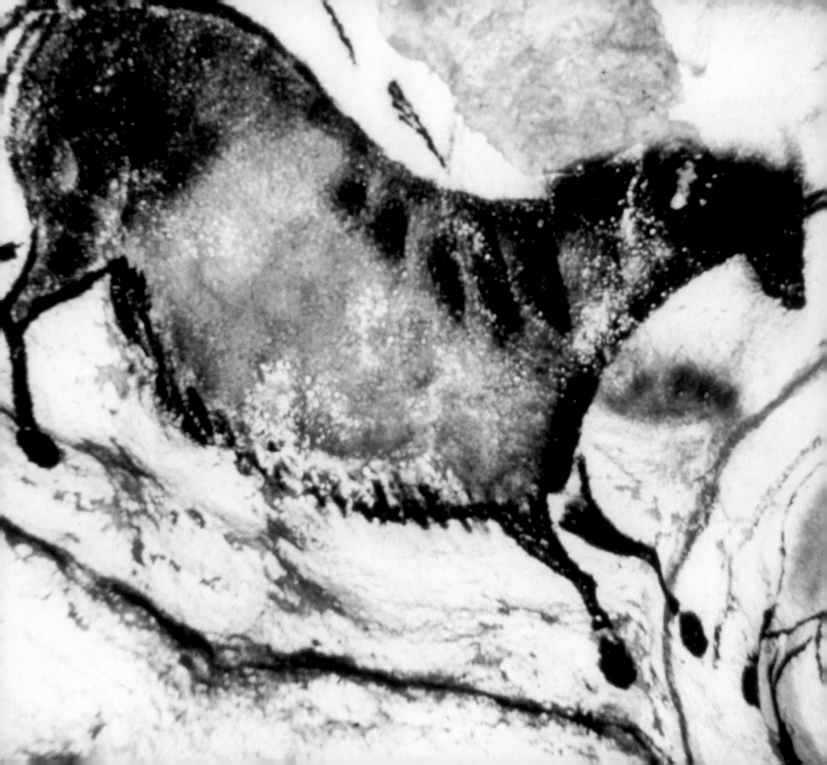

Many people think Appaloosas came from Spanish **explorers'** horses. Some of these horses had spots—and some got loose. Native Americans traded the horses throughout the West. In the 1700s, Nez Percé Indians began raising them. They kept only horses that were fast, strong, brave, and smart. Others were traded away. Not all of the Nez Percé's horses were spotted. But the spotted ones became the best known.

Some people believe that Appaloosas came from Russian horses instead. They think Russian fur traders brought some spotted horses to America.

Soon, people knew a Nez Percé horse when they saw one. The Nez Percé lived in Idaho and Washington. They were near the Palouse (pah-LOOS) River. People called a Nez Percé horse "a Palouse horse." Over time, the words turned into "Appaloosa."

◄ This is Chief Looking Glass. He was a Nez Percé chief in 1877.

In 1877, the U.S. army drove Nez Percé people from their homelands. Led by Chief Joseph, the Nez Percé headed for Canada. They rode over 1,300 miles (2,100 kilometers). Their fast, strong horses made them hard to catch. But the army caught them just outside Canada. The Nez Percé's horses were taken, given away, or left behind. The breed was almost lost.

In 1975, Appaloosas became the state horse of Idaho.

In the 1930s, some people became interested in Appaloosas again. They began to raise them. The Appaloosa Horse Club was started in 1938. This brought even more attention to the breed. Today, Appaloosas are well known and well loved.

These Appaloosas live on a horse farm. They have lots of space to run and play. You can really see the blanket pattern on the horse in front! ▶

WHAT ARE APPALOOSAS LIKE?

When strangers come near, Appaloosas sometimes get jumpy. But these horses like attention. If they feel safe, they are very friendly. And they are easy to handle.

Appaloosas are also smart and easy to train. Sometimes they can be stubborn. But most of them work very well with people.

These horses have lots of energy. They are strong and brave, too. And they are gentle and easygoing. They make good horses for young people or new riders.

Spending time with horses can help children with special needs. Gentle Appaloosas are good choices for this work.

This little girl is riding her family's Appaloosa. The horse knows the girl and feels safe with her. ▶

★★★ APPALOOSAS AT WORK

In the late 1800s and early 1900s, people in the West loved circuses. Appaloosas often starred in Western circus shows. These horses had a smooth **gait**. They could stop, start, and turn quickly. They could do different tricks. People liked them for rodeos and roundup work, too.

Today, Appaloosas are known as all-around horses. They are still used for calf roping. They do well in horse shows, too. Some are trained for jumping. Appaloosas' strength and **endurance** make them great for cross-country races. And lots of people ride Appaloosas just for fun.

Endurance racers go 25 to 100 miles (40 to 161 kilometers) in a single day! Some races are even longer. The horses might go 50 miles (80 kilometers) each day.

Some Appaloosas are trained to pull carriages. These horses are pulling carriages in New Jersey. ▶

★ ★ ★ APPALOOSAS TODAY

Years ago, Appaloosas were found only in North America. Now they are popular in other countries as well. There are Appaloosa horse clubs as far away as Australia. People raise Appaloosas in South America, too. The breed has become very popular in Europe. There, Appaloosas are often trained to race and hunt.

People are working to keep Appaloosas from getting mixed with other breeds. This will help Appaloosas keep their special look. It will also help them keep their spirit.

Some Appaloosas have a gait called the "Appaloosa **shuffle**." This smooth, tireless gait is something like a running walk. The legs on the same side move together.

This Appaloosa is enjoying a fall day on a horse farm. You can clearly see its leopard pattern. ▶

Lots of people like to race their Appaloosas. They tattoo a number on the inside of the horse's lip. That way no horse can be mistaken for another.

Appaloosas do not live everywhere in the world yet. But people are finding out what wonderful horses they are. Someday, Appaloosas might be found in every country.

If you see a spotted horse, take a look at its coat. What pattern does it have? Does the horse have striped hooves? Can you see the whites of its eyes? Now you can tell whether it belongs to this special breed!

◀ Even as the sun goes down, these Appaloosas continue to run and play. You can see how powerful they are.

★ ★ ★ BODY PARTS OF A HORSE

1. Ears
2. Forelock
3. Forehead
4. Eyes
5. Nostril
6. Lips
7. Muzzle
8. Chin
9. Cheek
10. Neck
11. Shoulder
12. Chest
13. Forearm
14. Knee
15. Cannon
16. Coronet
17. Hoof

28

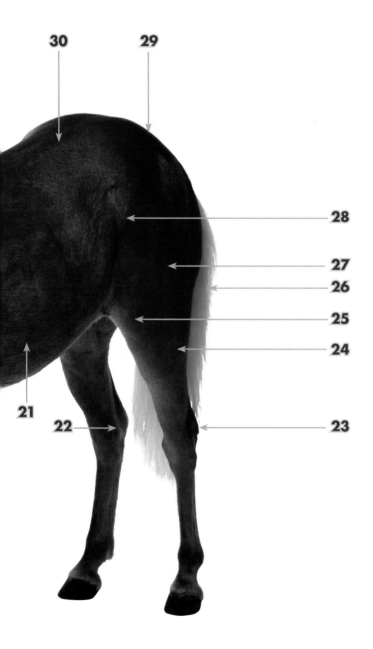

30

29

28

27

26

25

24

23

21

22

18. Pastern
19. Fetlock
20. Elbow
21. Barrel
22. Chestnut
23. Hock
24. Gaskin
25. Stifle
26. Tail
27. Thigh
28. Point of hip
29. Croup
30. Loin
31. Back
32. Withers
33. Mane
34. Poll

GLOSSARY

ancient (AYN-shunt) Something that is ancient is very old. Spotted horses are pictured in ancient art.

bay (BAY) A bay horse is brown with a black mane and tail. Some Appaloosas are bays.

breed (BREED) A breed is a certain type of an animal. Appaloosas are a colorful breed of horse.

endurance (in-DUR-untz) Endurance is being able to keep doing something that is very hard. Some Appaloosas take part in endurance races.

explorers (ex-PLOR-urz) Explorers travel to other places to see what they are like. Appaloosas might have come from Spanish explorers' horses.

foals (FOHLZ) Foals are baby horses. Appaloosa foals sometimes change color as they grow up.

gait (GATE) A gait is a way of walking or stepping. Appaloosas are known for their smooth gait.

mottled (MAH-tuld) Something that is mottled has spots or patches of color. Appaloosas have mottled skin.

roan (ROHN) Roan horses are a solid color with a few white hairs. Some Appaloosas are roans.

shuffle (SHUH-ful) A shuffle is a way of moving. You slide your feet along without lifting them high. Some Appaloosas have a special "Appaloosa shuffle."

withers (WIH-thurz) The withers is the highest part of a horse's back. An Appaloosa's height is measured at the withers.

TO FIND OUT MORE

In the Library

Gentle, Victor, and Janet Perry. *Appaloosas*. Milwaukee, WI: Gareth Stevens, 1998.

Patent, Dorothy Hinshaw, and William Muñoz (photographer).
Appaloosa Horses. New York: Holiday House, 1988.

Sharp, Thelma, and Georgia Graham (illustrator). *The Saturday Appaloosa*.
Calgary: Red Deer Press, 2001.

Stone, Lynn M. *Appaloosas*. Vero Beach, FL: Rourke, 1998.

On the Web

Visit our Web site for lots of links about Appaloosa horses:
http://www.childsworld.com/links

Note to Parents, Teachers, and Librarians: We routinely check our Web links
to make sure they're safe, active sites—so encourage your readers to check them out!

INDEX

About the author: Pamela Dell is the author of more than fifty books for young people. She likes writing about four-legged animals as well as insects, birds, famous people, and interesting times in history. She has published both fiction and nonfiction books and has also created several interactive computer games for kids. Pamela divides her time between Los Angeles, where the weather is mostly warm and sunny all year, and Chicago, where she loves how wildly the seasons change every few months.